How Our Nation Was Born: The American Revolution

By Carole Marsh

Editor: Chad Beard ● **Cover Design:** Victoria DeJoy ● **Design & Layout:** Cecil Anderson and Lynette Rowe

Gallopade is proud to be a member of these educational organizations and associations:

The National School Supply and Equipment Association (NSSEA)
National Association for Gifted Children (NAGC)
American Booksellers Association (ABA)
Association of Partners for Public Lands (APPL)
Museum Store Association (MSA)
Publishers Marketing Association (PMA)
International Reading Association (IRA)

Published by

GALLOPADE™
INTERNATIONAL
800-536-2GET
www.gallopade.com

Other Carole Marsh Books

Orville & Wilbur Wright . . . Step Out Into The Sky!
Lewis & Clark Go On a Hike: The Story of the Corps of Discovery
"What A Deal!": The Louisiana Purchase
How Our Nation Was Born: The American Revolution
When Brother Fought Brother: The American Civil War
The Fight For Equality: The U.S. Civil Rights Movement

State Stuff™, Available for all 50 states:

My First Pocket Guide
State My First Book
State Wheel of Fortune Gamebook
State Survivor Gamebook
State Illustrated Timelines
"Jography!": A Fun Run Through Our State

The State Coloring Book
The Big Reproducible Activity Book
State Millionaire Gamebook
State Project Books
Jeopardy: Answers & Questions About
    Our State

1,000 Readers™

Orville and Wilbur Wright
Louisiana Purchase
Benjamin Franklin
Martin Luther King, Jr

Meriwether Lewis & William Clark
George Washington
Ulysses S. Grant
Rosa Parks

Sacagawea
Paul Revere
Robert E. Lee
Thurgood Marshall

Patriotic Favorites™

Patriotic Favorites Coloring Book
Patriotic Biographies
The Daily Patriot: 365 Quotations

Young Patriots Coloring & Activity Book
Patriotic Projects
Patriotism: 365 Definitions

2

Table of Contents

©Carole Marsh/Gallopade International/800-536-2GET/www.gallopade.com/American Milestones/American Revolution

A Word From the Author

Dear Reader,

The American Revolution did not happen overnight. After the thirteen colonies were established, the colonists had plenty to do to keep themselves busy. They had come to this "New World" to make a place for themselves and were eager to get started. Many colonies set up their own representative governments. Of course the King was still in ultimate control.

War broke out between the colonists and the British in April, 1775. You remember the "shot heard 'round the world" when the war began in Lexington and Concord, Massachusetts. When the Continental Congress met, they told each colony to act as an independent state. Their only common goal was to be free from Great Britain, but this was common cause enough.

As the American Revolution got underway, it seemed logical to declare a formal separation from British rule. On July 4, 1776, a document called the Declaration of Independence did just that. Many colonists fought for their freedom. Some wanted to remain loyal to Britain. Some colonists were labeled traitors by both sides.

I hope that you have as much fun learning about the Revolutionary War as I had writing this book. I think you will find that there is a lot of interesting and true facts about this time in our nation's history.

Carole Marsh

"These are the times that try men's souls. The summer soldier and the sunshine patriot will, in this crisis, shrink from the service of their country; but he that stands it now, deserves the love and thanks of man and woman."
— Thomas Paine; The American Crisis

A Timeline of Events

March 5, 1770 — Soldiers kill five colonists in the Boston Massacre

December 16, 1773 — The Boston Tea Party

September 5–October 26, 1774 — First Continental Congress meets in Philadelphia, Pennsylvania

April 19, 1775 — Battles of Lexington and Concord

May 10, 1775 — Green Mountain Boys capture British Fort Ticonderoga

June 15, 1775 — Congress names George Washington as Commander-in-Chief of the Continental Army

June 17, 1775 — Battle of Breed's Hill and Bunker Hill

December 31, 1775 — American Army invades Canada and tries to take Quebec but fails

January 1776 — Thomas Paine publishes Common Sense

July 4, 1776 — Declaration of Independence

December 25–January 3, 1776–77 — Americans cross the Delaware and defeat the British at the Battles of Trenton and Princeton, New Jersey

December 19, 1777 — American Army spends the winter at Valley Forge

September 1779 — John Paul Jones' Bonhomme Richard captures the British Serapis

January 17, 1781 — British defeated at Cowpens, South Carolina

October 19, 1781 — Cornwallis surrenders at Yorktown, Virginia

September 3, 1783 — Treaty of Peace of Paris

5

How Our Nation was Born:
The American Revolution

6

During the American Revolution, thirteen British colonies broke away from Great Britain. The colonists wanted to be free from rules they felt were unfair. There were some who wanted to remain loyal to Great Britain. But many Americans fought bravely to win their freedom from Great Britain.

When the smoke cleared and the war was over, the separate colonies were combined to form one nation. The United States of America was born!

The Boston Massacre: March 5, 1770

Crispus Attucks was a very large man for his day. He stood over six feet tall and had a sturdy build. He was of mixed African and American Indian descent. Attucks was born into slavery in Massachusetts. He was still a boy in 1750 when he ran away and worked as a sailor spending most of his time at sea. In 1770, Attucks was living in Boston, Massachusetts. He went by the name of Michael Johnson so that no one would know he was a runaway slave.

The British Army had occupied Boston since 1768. They were trying to enforce British laws. Fights broke out between British soldiers and sailors and dockworkers almost every day. On March 5, Attucks and many others carried pieces of firewood clubs and began threatening the soldiers near the Customs House in Boston. The frightened soldiers reacted by firing their muskets into the angry mob killing Attucks and two others instantly. Two more later died from their wounds.

The soldiers were freed after a trial, but the rest of the British soldiers were withdrawn from the city. Paul Revere, a patriot, made a famous picture he titled, "The Boston Massacre." In it he showed Attucks lying dead. The death of Attucks inspired others to start the American Revolution.

Fact or Opinion

Label each of these statements. Write F next to each statement that is a fact. Write O next to each statement that is an opinion.

_____ 1. Crispus Attucks was born into slavery.

_____ 2. British soldiers should not have come to Boston.

_____ 3. Crispus Attucks was killed at the Boston Massacre.

_____ 4. Paul Revere made a picture of the Boston Massacre.

_____ 5. The United States is the best country to live in.

_____ 6. British soldiers should not have fired at the angry mob.

FAST FACT! John Adams was the lawyer for soldiers on trial for the Boston Massacre.

8

December 16, 1773: Boston Tea Party

The East India Company was the only company allowed to ship tea to the colonies. Massachusetts Governor Thomas Hutchinson was an investor in the company and would make a profit on any tea sold in the colonies. Patriots in Boston refused to buy the tea because they thought it was unfair that only one company could sell the tea. Patriots were willing to pay more for tea that was smuggled into the country illegally than drink the tea of the East India Company. They were really mad!

On the night of December 16, 1773, a group called the "Sons of Liberty" dressed as Indians and headed for Griffin's Wharf where the cargo of tea waited. The men boarded three ships, pulled out the tea chests, broke them open, and dumped all the tea chests into Boston Harbor. They called it "making saltwater tea." When the tide went out of Boston Harbor, it carried 342 chests of tea with it.

Make this tasty treat and share with a friend!

Cut out

Boston Tea Party Popcorn

Ingredients:
- 2 1/2 quarts popped popcorn
- 1/4 cup melted butter
- 2 tablespoons instant lemon-flavored iced tea mix
- 1 tablespoon granulated sugar

Directions:
Put freshly-popped popcorn in a large bowl. Drizzle butter over it and toss. Combine tea and sugar. Add to buttered popcorn and toss again.

Note: Preparation of "Boston Tea Party Popcorn" should be carried out under the supervision of an adult.

9

Paul Revere's Ride

Paul Revere was a patriot and a silversmith. He was a leader in the Boston Sons of Liberty, and made a famous picture of the Boston Massacre. He also helped plan the Boston Tea Party.

On the night of April 18, 1775, Paul Revere, William Dawes, and Dr. Samuel Prescott set out on horseback. They were riding from Boston to Concord by way of Medford and Lexington. The truth is that Revere may have never shouted "The British are coming," but he was riding to warn John Hancock and Samuel Adams that they were about to be arrested by the British Army. Revere also wanted to warn colonists in Concord that an important store of weapons was going to be seized. Hancock and Adams did escape the British and the colonists in Concord hid their stash of weapons.

Many years later in 1863, Henry Wadsworth Longfellow published a poem about Paul Revere. The famous poem made Revere a legend.

Excerpt from *"The Midnight Ride of Paul Revere"* by Henry Wadsworth Longfellow

Listen my children and you shall hear
Of the midnight ride of Paul Revere,
On the eighteenth of April, in Seventy-five;
Hardly a man is now alive
Who remembers that famous day and year.

He said to his friend, "If the British march
By land or sea from the town to-night,
Hang a lantern aloft in the belfry arch
Of the North Church tower as a signal light,—
One if by land, and two if by sea;
And I on the opposite shore will be,
Ready to ride and spread the alarm
Through every Middlesex village and farm,
For the country folk to be up and to arm."

Answer the questions below!

1. How many lanterns were to be used if the British were coming by sea? _____

2. Who was Paul Revere trying to warn? _____

3. Would you make a "midnight ride" to warn your friends of trouble? _____

10

The Shot Heard 'Round the World': April 19, 1775, Lexington and Concord

Minutemen line the field green at Lexington. They know that the British are on their way to Concord and they are outnumbered 10 to 1. But the patriots stand their ground determined to protect their rights. When the smoke clears, eight dead patriots lie on Lexington Green; ten wounded have escaped. Only one British private received a minor leg wound. The Battle of Lexington is over.

Couriers spread the news of the Battle of Lexington. Church bells ring and drums beat a warning to the colonists: the British are coming! About 150 Minutemen rush to meet the approaching British force, but when they meet, they decide to march back to Concord. When the British begin to set fire to the town, the patriots decide to make a stand, but not to fire unless fired upon. The British fired first and the Patriots returned their fire. Then the Battle of Concord seemed to fizzle out.

What happened next both surprised and scared the British soldiers. They began a retreat to Charlestown. All along the way, patriots rushed ahead of them and hid behind rocks, trees, buildings, or whatever. Hundreds of other patriots from all around the region join in the fight. The British soldiers hurried to the safety of hills outside of Charlestown known as Breed's and Bunker. They collapse exhausted knowing they are safe here protected by guns on the king's ships in the Charles River.

Circle the characteristics below that you would find in Minutemen.

slow   scared   weak

patriotic   foolish   confused

confident

lazy   brave

11

Native Americans

Native Americans fought with both the patriots and the British during the American Revolution. Most American Indians were concerned for their own people and their own way of life. Both patriots and the British made promises to Indian tribes in order that they would fight with one side or another. Some Indian tribes remained neutral.

Dragging Canoe was a Cherokee Indian who accepted weapons from the British. In July 1776, Dragging Canoe's warriors attacked two American settlements in present-day Tennessee. He led many attacks during the rest of the American Revolution, but finally agreed to peace in 1784.

Make your own canoe like one that might have belonged to Dragging Canoe!

❶ Fold an 8.5x11" piece of paper (use any color) in half. Make a sharp crease.

❷ Make a 1/4" fold from the creased edge to one side, then fold it to the other side.

❸ Fold the open edges back to the 1/4" crease mark.

❹ Fold both edges up so the "W" shape is at the bottom and lay flat.

❺ Fold the corners up to about 1/2" from the top. Reverse the folds.

❻ Make a 1/4" fold from top edge that stops just above the corner fold. Make another 1/4" that folds over the corner fold. Repeat on the other side. Make all creases sharp.

❼ Use your fingers to push out the crease at the bottom of your canoe. This creates a hull and allows your canoe to float. Add the cut-out figure of Dragging Canoe.

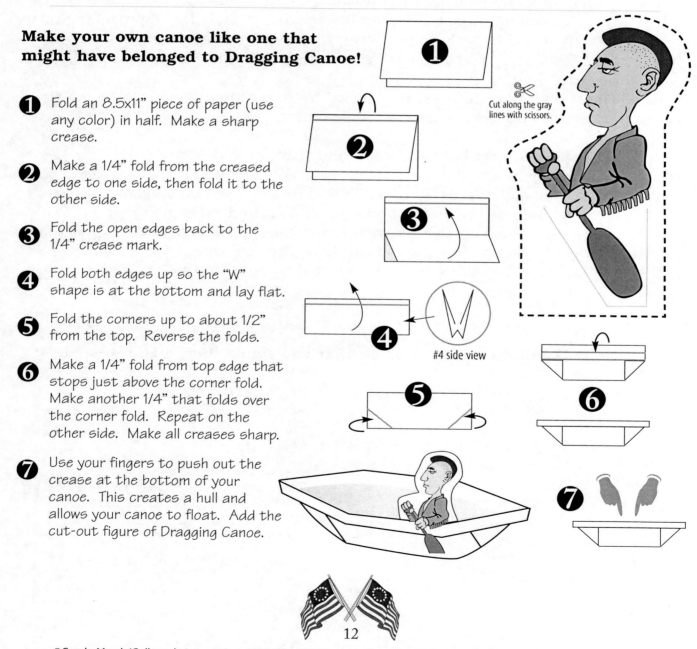

Cut along the gray lines with scissors.

#4 side view

George Washington

George Washington began his military career during the French and Indian War. He distinguished himself by leading the Virginia militia against the French. As a former surveyor, Washington was valuable to the British Army as someone who knew the land well. However, Washington felt like he was not appreciated by the British.

As a member of the Virginia House of Burgesses from 1759–1774, Washington was against many of the taxes imposed by the British government. He was a delegate to the first Continental Congress. The second Continental Congress met May 10, 1775, just a few weeks after Lexington and Concord. The British government declared the people of Massachusetts had committed treason. Washington appeared at the meeting wearing his uniform from the French and Indian War! He was ready to fight the British, defend the patriots of Massachusetts, and win the American Revolution! During this meeting, Washington was elected general and commander-in-chief.

During the revolution, Washington organized the army, recruited and trained a second army, and established the first American navy. He also worked to keep patriots focused on their main cause. Washington kept the peace when army officers threatened to march on the capital because they had not received their full pay.

Cherry Thumbprint Cookies

Cut out

Ingredients:
- 1 teaspoon vanilla
- 2 egg yolks
- 2 cups flour
- maraschino cherries
- 2 sticks butter or margarine
- 1/2 cup brown sugar
- 1/2 teaspoon salt

Directions:
Preheat oven to 350 degrees. In a large bowl, mix together the vanilla, butter, egg yolks and brown sugar until creamy. Add the flour and salt and mix well. Roll the dough into 1 inch balls and place them on greased cookie sheets. Have the children make a thumbprint in each ball and then place a maraschino cherry in each thumbprint. Bake for 8 to 10 minutes. Makes about 3 dozen cookies.

Note: Preparation of "Cherry Thumbprint Cookies" should be carried out under the supervision of an adult.

13

Declaration of Independence

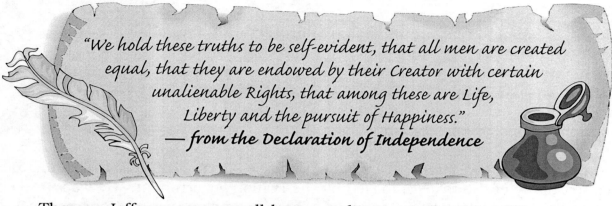

"We hold these truths to be self-evident, that all men are created equal, that they are endowed by their Creator with certain unalienable Rights, that among these are Life, Liberty and the pursuit of Happiness."
— *from the Declaration of Independence*

Thomas Jefferson was a well-known politician at the time of the American Revolution. He became governor of Virginia during the war. He wrote many important documents, including the Virginia Declaration of Rights, the Virginia Statute for Religious Freedom, and the Declaration of Independence.

Benjamin Franklin and John Adams helped make a few changes to Jefferson's first draft of the Declaration of Independence. Then it went to Congress where a few other small changes were made. Then finally on July 4, 1776, Congress adopted the Declaration of Independence. Today, Americans celebrate the birth of our nation every year on the Fourth of July!

The document is a statement or a "declaration" of freedom or "independence" from British rule. There is also a list of things that colonists felt were unfair things that King George III had done that made colonists angry.

Most of the representatives signed the Declaration of Independence on August 2, 1776. The reason they waited so long was that it was sent out to be printed on parchment. Parchment is made of animal skin and lasts much longer than paper.

The first and largest signature is that of John Hancock, president of the Continental Congress.

Practice writing your "John Hancock" below. (John Hancock can also mean signature.)

_____

_____

_____

Yankee Doodle

Tradition has it that Yankee Doodle had its origins in the French and Indian War when New England troops joined Braddock's forces at Niagara. Unlike the professional British army, the colonials were a rough bunch, some wearing buckskins and furs. Dr. Richard Schuckburg, a British Army surgeon, is said to have written the tune ridiculing the Americans in the early 1750s.

Despite the fact it began as ridicule, the colonials took the song for their own. Countless verses were written, many of which made fun of their officers, including George Washington. When Cornwallis surrendered at Yorktown it is said while the British played "The World Turned Upside Down," the Americans played "Yankee Doodle."

During Pre-Revolutionary America when the song "Yankee Doodle" first became popular, the word *macaroni* in the line that reads "stuck a feather in his hat and called it macaroni" didn't refer to pasta. Instead, "Macaroni" was a fancy and overdressed "dandy" style of Italian clothing widely imitated in England at the time. So by just sticking a feather in his cap and calling himself a "Macaroni," Yankee Doodle was proudly proclaiming himself to be a country bumpkin, because that was how the English regarded most colonials at that time.

 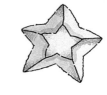

Yankee Doodle

Yankee Doodle went to town
riding on a pony.
Stuck a feather in his cap
and called it Macaroni!

Chorus
Yankee doodle, keep it up
Yankee doodle dandy
Mind the music and the step
And with the girls be handy.

The Guns of Fort Ticonderoga

On May 10, 1775, Ethan Allen and the Green Mountain Boys captured Fort Ticonderoga in northeastern New York without firing a single shot! They captured another British outpost at Crown Point, and a British ship on the Canadian Richelieu River. This was the first colonial victory of the war. Ethan Allen then attempted an assault on Montreal. He was captured and imprisoned by the British where he remained for the rest of the war.

Later in the war, Colonel Henry Knox and his troops transported about fifty pieces of artillery more than 300 miles to help General Washington in Boston. Knox and his men moved these heavy cannons and other guns without any wagons or roads! Instead they used flat-bottom boats and sleds hauled by horse and oxen.

In the 1920s, New York State decided the path taken by Knox and his men should be marked with stone monuments. Thirty of them mark the trail known today as the Knox Trail.

Connect the monuments (dots) to find the trail.

The Green Mountain Boys earned their nickname from the New York threat to drive Vermont settlers off the fields and "into the Green Mountains."

George Washington wrote of Ethan Allen, "There is an original something about him that commands attention."

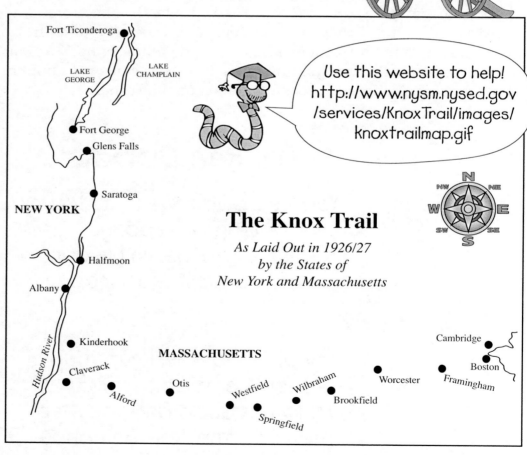

Use this website to help!
http://www.nysm.nysed.gov/services/KnoxTrail/images/knoxtrailmap.gif

The Knox Trail

As Laid Out in 1926/27 by the States of New York and Massachusetts

Fort Ticonderoga
LAKE GEORGE
LAKE CHAMPLAIN
Fort George
Glens Falls
Saratoga
NEW YORK
Halfmoon
Albany
Hudson River
Kinderhook
Claverack
Alford
Otis
MASSACHUSETTS
Westfield
Springfield
Wilbraham
Brookfield
Worcester
Framingham
Cambridge
Boston

Benedict Arnold — Lost Treasure

Benedict Arnold was one of the best generals in the American Army, and one of the worst traitors. He was with Ethan Allen at Fort Ticonderoga and helped defeat the British at the second Battle of Saratoga. Then it was discovered that he had been selling information to the British for a year and a half! After that, the British Army made him a brigadier general. He continued to fight in the war — now for the other side! Not many people on either side thought very much of Benedict Arnold. After the war, he lived in Canada where he tried to make money but was not successful. He died deeply in debt in London.

Lost Treasure

In an effort to attack the British at Quebec during the Revolution in 1775, Colonel Benedict Arnold was given a war chest full of gold coins and a group of men to make their way through the Maine wilderness to Quebec. Rain and snow made the rivers treacherous, and somewhere along either the Dead River or below a waterfall on the Chadiere River, the gold-filled paychest containing $50,000 was lost!

Answer the following question.

Would you become a traitor and "sell out" your friends for money? Why or why not?

_____

_____

_____

_____

Today if you call someone "Benedict Arnold" you're calling them a traitor.

17

Valley Forge

On December 19, 1777, Washington and the Continental Army arrived at Valley Forge, Pennsylvania. Finally on January 13, 1778, Washington's men completed

the last of the log huts that would house them for the remainder of the winter. Washington promised his troops that he would suffer along with them and stayed in a tent until most of the huts were built. The army at the camp numbered about 11,000, only 8,200 of them fit for duty.

Washington sent letters to Congress asking them to provide food and clothing. Many of his men lacked hats, shoes, and coats. They went many days without meat. A meal might have consisted of firecake (a thin bread of flour and water baked over a campfire) and water, and sometimes even the firecake was scarce.

Washington's army suffered terribly from cold, hunger, exposure, and disease. Possibly 2,500 perished during the six months at camp. But plans were made to reorganize the supply services. Drill and training were directed by Baron von Steuben, formerly of the Prussian Army. By spring, the American Army was reinvigorated.

Firecake Recipe

Firecake is a mixture of flour and water — and salt if the soldiers happened to have it. You mix the ingredients together, form it into a cake, and bake it on a rock in the fire or over the fire, usually in the ashes until blackened. You can make a form of it at home by taking some flour and a little salt and mixing it with water until you make a thick, damp dough. You don't want it to be too sticky. Form it into a flat cake in the palm of your hand and put it on a greased cookie sheet and bake until brown. You could also just drop "globs" of the dough onto the cookie sheet and let them bake like cookies. The final product will be a very hard, not very tasty "biscuit" that served as food for the soldiers during the Revolutionary War when their regular rations were not available.

Note: Preparation of "Firecakes" should be carried out under the supervision of an adult.

The Hessians!

To help out the British Army in America, the British government paid money for the services of 30,000 German soldiers. Seventeen thousand soldiers were obtained from the principality of Hesse, and the term Hessians was applied to all the German soldiers. Of their number, 7,500 died in America and 5,000 deserted!

In December of 1776, George Washington was aware that the British had gone into winter quarters. He led 2,400 patriots across the Delaware River on the night of December 25, 1776. Washington knew the Hessians would be up late celebrating the Christmas holiday. The next morning, the patriots surprised a Hessian garrison of 1,500 men at Trenton, New Jersey. Of these, more than 900 were captured. The surprise attack worked — and the Americans only suffered 4 wounded.

Then on January 3, 1777, General Washington won another important battle at Princeton, New Jersey. This victory along with the win at Trenton greatly improved morale in the American Army. They were finally winning!

List some of the reasons Americans chose to fight for their freedom. Make a placard by punching holes in the top corners of two pieces of poster-board. Connect them with string. Leave an approximate 18 inches of string between the matching holes on each sheet. Dress up for this era and march around wearing your placards!

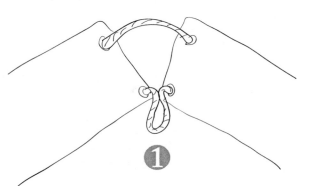

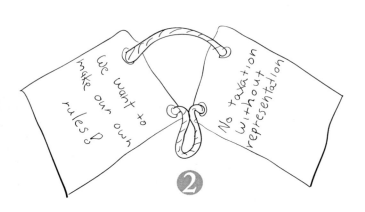

Francis Marion "The Swamp Fox"

Francis Marion was born and raised in South Carolina. At the beginning of the war, he was both a delegate to the state provincial congress and a captain in the militia. By 1776, he rose to the rank of major. He worked well with other American officers. Then in 1780, Marion broke his ankle in an accident. He had left the fort in Charleston to recover before the city was captured by the British. South Carolinians were defenseless with no American Army left in the state!

Marion then organized troops of volunteer soldiers. They lived and stayed mostly in the thick swamps. They moved often and were very successful at attacking British soldiers because they were quick and moved without being noticed. He became known as "The Swamp Fox" because of his tactics. Marion helped American Armies when they finally returned to South Carolina.

Write the name of these animals that Francis Marion shared the swamp with.

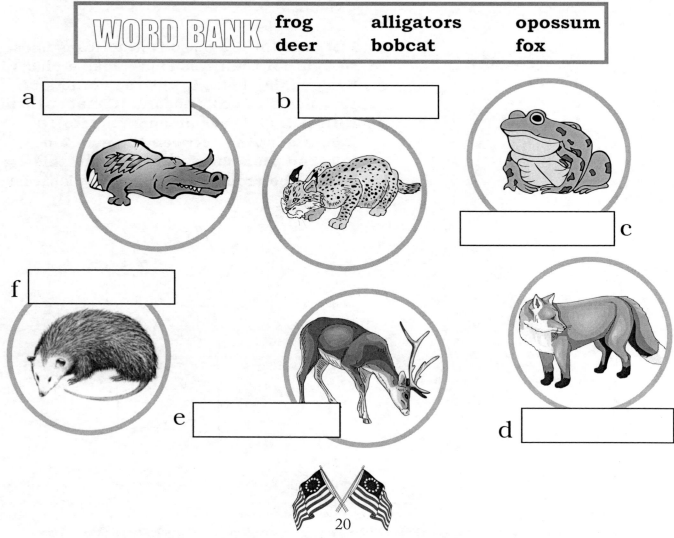

WORD BANK

frog	alligators	opossum
deer	bobcat	fox

The Stars and Stripes

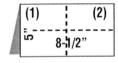

BETSY ROSS worked as a seamstress and upholsterer, carrying on her husband's upholstery business after he was killed in the American Revolution. According to legend, in 1776 she was visited by George Washington, Robert Morris, and her husband's uncle George Ross, who asked her to make a flag for the new nation based on a sketch by Washington. She is supposed also to have suggested the use of the five-pointed star rather than the six-pointed one chosen by Washington.

FRANCIS HOPKINSON was a musician, a Congressman from New Jersey, and a signer of the Declaration of Independence. The journals of the Continental Congress recorded debate on whether or not he should have been paid for the design of the Stars and Stripes. The debate was not on whether he designed the flag — they argued about how much and whether or not it should be shared with others. At any rate, Hopkinson was not paid for the design, but there is plenty of evidence that he helped with it.

FIVE-POINTED STARS!

STEP 1

Fold an 8-1/2-by-10-inch piece of paper in half. Leave it folded and then fold it in half from top to bottom and again from side to side. When you unfold it, you should see a cross.

STEP 2

Take the upper left corner (1) and fold it from the center of the top to the crease on the horizontal line. Now take corner 1 and fold it back to the left until it lines up with the left side.

STEP 3

Take the top right corner (2) and fold it over to the left. Then bring corner 2 back to the right and fold it again. The paper now looks a little like a necktie.

STEP 4

With scissors, make a cut from corner 2 across the paper to a point about 1 inch down from the top point. When you unfold this snippet it should be a perfect five-pointed star just like Betsy made!

The story of Betsy Ross was not made public until 1870 when her grandson, William J. Canby told the story passed on through his family. Though Ross did make flags for the navy, no firm evidence supports the legend of the national flag.

Make a bunch and hang them all around!

21

The World Turned Upside Down!

The last major battle of the Revolutionary War was fought in 1781 at Yorktown. Lord Cornwallis had made a camp there with 7,000 troops. Attempting to save him, a British fleet of 19 ships sailed to Chesapeake Bay, where Admiral de Grasse and a French fleet of 28 ships engaged them on September 5, and turned them back. By September 28, Washington had covered Yorktown on the land-side with 17,000 French and American troops. All hope of escape gone, Cornwallis and over 7,000

British troops surrendered on October 19. Lord Cornwallis asked for his troops to be paroled and returned to England, but Washington demanded unconditional surrender. Many consider this surrender as the end of the Revolutionary War.

As the stunned British soldiers gave up their weapons, it has been said that British fife and drums played a tune called "The World Turned Upside Down." There is much debate about whether or not this tune was actually played. However, the world had been turned upside down. The ideas of the patriots and the newly formed government seemed strange to many and would change the world forever!

Read the information above and answer the following questions.

1. How many more ships did the French fleet have than the British fleet?

   _____

2. How many more troops did Washington have than Cornwallis?

   _____

3. How many years had it taken to fight the war? (Hint: It began in 1775.)

   _____

4. How many days passed between the day the French fleet engaged the British and the day Washington covered Yorktown on the land-side?

   _____

5. How many British troops surrendered on October 19, 1781?

   _____

22

1783 Treaty of Paris

After 1778, the war went badly for England. But King George III refused to consider peace negotiations even when news of Cornwallis' surrender at Yorktown reached London in November 1781. Finally in March 1782, the king accepted the fact that the colonies were lost.

Benjamin Franklin acted for America in the early stages of the negotiations with the British. He was later joined by John Adams, John Jay, and Henry Laurens. The negotiations then began to move toward a final settlement. On November 30, 1782, the preliminary peace treaty was signed, and on September 3, 1783, the treaty (called the Peace of Paris) became final.

The American Revolution lasted eight long years and many lives were lost. **Write down how you think each person felt on September 3, 1783.**

KING GEORGE III _____

_____

GENERAL WASHINGTON _____

_____

LORD CORNWALLIS _____

_____

A BRITISH SOLDIER _____

_____

AN AMERICAN SOLDIER _____

_____

Proclaim Liberty Across the Land!

The Liberty Bell is an important symbol of the United States. For many people it represents freedom or "liberty." Today you can visit the Liberty Bell at Independence National Historical Park in Philadelphia, Pennsylvania. There is a special Liberty Bell Center where the Bell is on display. Read more about the Liberty Bell.

April 1775 — It rang to announce the Battle of Lexington and Concord.

July 4, 1776 — The Liberty Bell did not ring on July 4, 1776 for the Declaration of Independence. The reason? The Declaration is dated July 4, 1776, but on that day, the Declaration was sent to the printer! Read on.

July 8, 1776 — The first public reading of the Declaration of Independence. Bells tolled throughout the city on that day. Tradition holds that the Liberty Bell rang out this day. However, the steeple was in bad condition and historians doubt the likelihood of the story.

September 1777 — The British were set to move into Philadelphia. Philadelphians tried to remove anything the British could make use of, including bells. Bells could be melted down and recast into cannonballs. The bell was hidden in the basement of a church in Allentown.

June 27, 1778 — The Bell was brought back to Philadelphia but not rehung. The rotten steeple wouldn't hold it. The Bell was stored for seven years. Some believe the Bell was stored in one of the munitions sheds that flanked the State House.

1781 — The State House steeple was torn down.

1785 — The Bell was rehung in the rebuilt State House steeple.

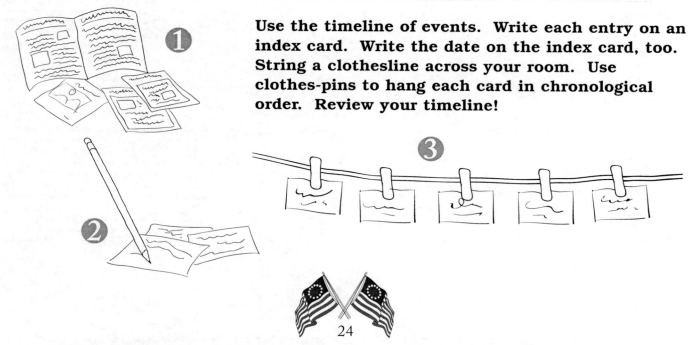

Use the timeline of events. Write each entry on an index card. Write the date on the index card, too. String a clothesline across your room. Use clothes-pins to hang each card in chronological order. Review your timeline!

24

Revolutionary Uniforms

Patriot Uniforms

The Minutemen who were ready at a minute's notice wore their regular clothes. Many of them probably wore three-cornered felt hats. Most wore short breeches and stockings instead of pants. No uniforms were worn by the patriots who fired the first shots at Lexington and Concord.

As the war progressed the Continental Army did have a uniform. It was mostly blue faced with red. Many of the state militias also had their own uniforms which were quite different from each other.

British Uniforms

British regulars wore uniforms that were mostly red. A nasty nickname for British soldiers during the American Revolution was "lobster-backs." They were more often called "redcoats."

Of course different regiments and different ranks had different uniforms as well. For example, officers often wore a short sword called a "hanger" which hung to the side of their uniform. Mounted officers could wear longer swords that wouldn't touch the ground because they were usually on their horses.

Make a patriotic hat!

Get a large piece of newspaper. Fold down one end to make a perfect square and cut away the excess piece. Then fold the square in half. Leave a one-inch strip at the bottom (along the open end). Fold the two upper corners inward and down to form a triangle. Fold the one-inch bottom strip up on both sides to form the brim of your general's hat!

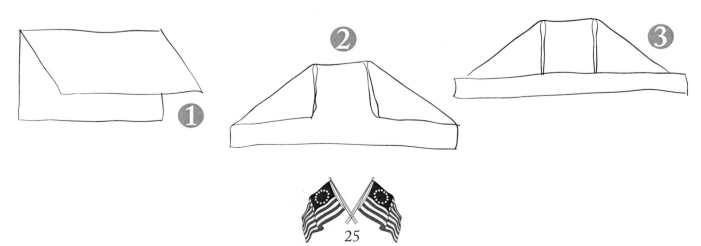

In the Navy

On Sept. 23, 1779, John Paul Jones and his ship the *Bon Homme Richard* encountered the ship *Serapis* and a smaller warship. Despite the superiority of the *Serapis*, Jones did not hesitate to attack. Jones sailed close in and finally in the battle tied the *Bon Homme Richard* to the British ship. Both ships were heavily damaged. The *Serapis* was on fire in at least 12 different places. The hull of the *Bon Homme Richard* was pierced, her decks were ripped, her hold was filling with water, and fires were destroying her; yet when the British captain asked if Jones was ready to surrender, the answer came proudly, "Sir, I have not yet begun to fight." When the *Serapis* surrendered, Jones and his men boarded her while his own vessel sank!

Which Way Did He Go?

Ships at sea often rely on a compass. A compass is a device used to find one of four directions (north, south, east, and west). This is done with a magnetic needle that freely turns on a pivot and points to the magnetic north. When you can see where north lies, you will know where the other directions are.

Make your own compass with a few simple materials.

Materials: magnet, cork, large sewing needle, plastic cup filled with water

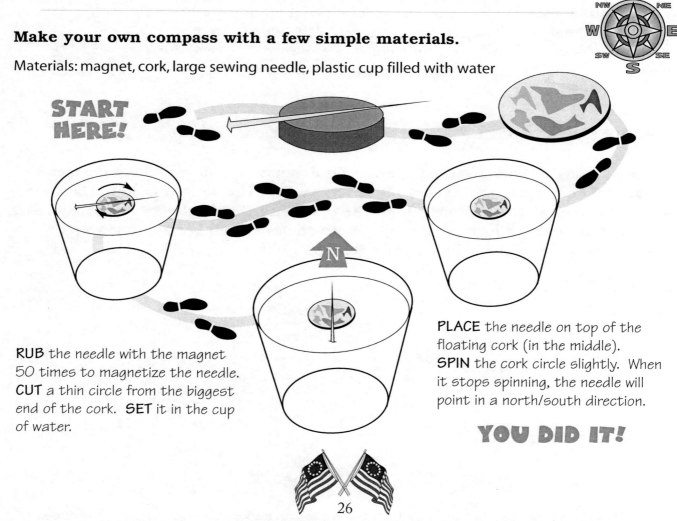

START HERE!

RUB the needle with the magnet 50 times to magnetize the needle. **CUT** a thin circle from the biggest end of the cork. **SET** it in the cup of water.

PLACE the needle on top of the floating cork (in the middle). **SPIN** the cork circle slightly. When it stops spinning, the needle will point in a north/south direction.

YOU DID IT!

Revolutionary Spies

One form of secret writing used by both the British and American armies during the American Revolution was invisible ink. Invisible ink, at the time of the Revolutionary War, usually consisted of a mixture of ferrous sulfate and water. The secret writing was placed between the lines of another letter, just in case they were caught by the enemy army, and could be read by treating the letter with heat by placing the paper over the flame of a candle or by treating it with another chemical such as sodium carbonate. John André gave instructions to British spies to mark their letters written in invisible ink with a "F" for fire and "A" for acid, so that the reader knew whether to use heat or a chemical solution to read the letter.

Letters written in invisible ink needed special care; water or other liquids could smear the invisible ink and make it impossible to read. The American Army used invisible ink frequently to report to George Washington. There are some examples in the Library of Congress' collection of Washington's papers.

Imagine you are a spy for the American Army. You have just discovered important information and need to write a message to General Washington. Remember, British troops are everywhere and you may be searched if stopped.

Write your secret message using these instructions! (Ask an adult for help!)

1. Take a toothpick and dip it in some lemon juice. Be sure to dip frequently.

2. Carefully "write" your message on a piece of paper and let it dry.

3. Heat the paper over a source of warm air such as a hair drier or a heat duct.

4. Read your secret message!

Patriot spy Nathan Hale was executed at the young age of 21. He was wearing a disguise instead of his uniform when General Howe discovered he was a spy. A witness to his execution reported that he made a speech ending with, "I only regret that I have but one life to lose for my country."

Women in the War

While many women stayed at home and tended to businesses or farms, many others went off to war. Many worked around the camps and a few even helped fight!

Molly Pitcher

Margaret Ludwig Hayes McCauley was among many women who were nicknamed "Molly Pitcher." These women were called this because they brought pitchers of water to men in the heat of battle. On June 28, 1778 at the Battle of Monmouth in New Jersey, her husband collapsed in battle either wounded or exhausted. Mary took his place as cannon loader for the rest of the fight, helping to keep the gun in action. In 1822, the Pennsylvania legislature voted to pay her a pension "for her services during the revolutionary war."

Captain Molly

Margaret Corbin earned this nickname. During the battle of Fort Washington in November 1776, her husband was killed while operating his gun, and Margaret stepped forward to take his place. She was severely wounded in the action and captured with the rest of the garrison. She was awarded half-pay for life by Congress in 1779 and is now buried at West Point.

Edenton Ladies Tea Party

Many women took the lead in the boycott of English goods. A group in North Carolina were nicknamed the Edenton Ladies Tea Party when they signed a pledge to support colonial resistance to British measures, including a continued boycott of tea. This was one of the earliest organized efforts on the part of women to influence public policy.

Washington's Sewing Circle

In the 1700s, politics was thought to be improper for women to be involved, but the American Revolution urged women to take part. The first nationwide women's organization, The Ladies Association, was organized during the war in Philadelphia by Esther de Berdt Reed. It raised money for Washington's army and was known as "Washington's Sewing Circle."

Legendary Leaders

Thomas Jefferson — Philosopher of the Revolution

Samuel Adams — Political Organizer

George Washington — Military Genius

Patrick Henry — The Orator

King George III — King of England

Charles Cornwallis — British General

Ethan Allen — Green Mountain Boys Leader

Crispus Attucks — Boston Massacre Martyr

Margaret Corbin — Captain Molly

Benjamin Franklin — Revolutionary Diplomat

Nathan Hale — Patriot Spy

Mary Ludwig Hays — Molly Pitcher

Francis Marion — The Swamp Fox

Thomas Paine — Writer and Soldier

Bio Bottles

Biography bottles are 2 liter bottles, emptied and cleaned. They are then decorated like your favorite Revolutionary War character. They can represent either someone who supported either the Americans or the British. Use your imagination.

Here are some items you may want to help you:
- 2 liter bottles
- glue
- paint
- fabric for clothes
- scissors
- felt
- yarn for hair
- balloon or Styrofoam ball for head

Additional Resources

WEBSITE

The National Society of the Sons of the American Revolution

www.sar.org

The Pennsylvania Society of Sons of the Revolution

www.amrev.org

BOOKS

John Paul Jones: Sailor, Hero, Father of the American Navy by Evan Thomas

Johnny Tremain by Esther Forbes

STATUE

A statue of Commodore John Barry stands in Independence Square on the south side of Independence Hall.

HOMES

Mount Vernon was the name of George Washington's home.

www.mountvernon.org

Red Hill was the name of Patrick Henry's home.

www.redhill.org

Monticello was the name of Thomas Jefferson's home.

www.monticello.org

Betsy Ross House

www.betsyrosshouse.org

Glossary

armistice: when both sides agree to stop fighting during a big war

boycott: to join with others and refuse to buy, sell, or use something; refusing to buy a product to show disapproval of a company

breeches: short pants, reaching just below the knees

customhouse: building where customs and duties (taxes) are paid or collected

delegate: a person sent to speak and act for others; a representative; a person given power or authority to act for others; representative

martyr: person who suffers or dies rather than give up his beliefs

mercenary: a soldier hired to fight for the army of a foreign country

morale: the moral or mental condition of a person or group with regard to cheerfulness and confidence

Parliament: ruling body of England (like our Congress)

patriot: person who shows great love and loyalty for his or her country

revolution: a battle or war fought by a group to gain independence; to overthrow a government

treason: betraying one's country; attempt to overthrow the government; the act or an instance of betraying one's country

31

Answer Key

Page 8: 1.F; 2.O; 3.F; 4.F; 5.O; 6.O

Page 10: 1. 2 lanterns; 2. Colonists in Concord, John Hancock, and Samuel Adams; 3. Answers will vary.

Page 11: patriotic, confident, brave

Page 17: Answers will vary

Page 20: a. alligators; b. bobcat; c. frog; d. fox; e. deer; f. opossum

Page 22: 1. 9 ships; 2. 10,000 troops; 3. 6 years; 4. 23 days; 5. Over 7,000 troops

Index

©Carole Marsh/Gallopade International/800-536-2GET/www.gallopade.com/American Milestones/American Revolution